GREEN EDITION®

At Dover Publications we'
earth-friendly manner and to h
Manufacturing books in the United Stat
eliminates the need for international fre
And printing on recycled paper helps mi...

The text of this book was printed on paper made with 10% post-consumer waste and the cover was printed on paper made with 10% post-consumer waste. At Dover, we use Environmental Defense's Paper Calculator to measure the benefits of these choices, including: the number of trees saved, gallons of water conserved, as well as air emissions and solid waste eliminated.

Courier Corporation, the manufacturer of this book, owns the Green Edition Trademark.

Please visit the product page for *Day of the Dead Clip Art for Machine Embroidery* at www.doverpublications.com to see a detailed account of the environmental savings we've achieved over the life of this book.

Day of the Dead Clip Art for Machine Embroidery

Manufactured in the United States by Courier Corporation
99202001
www.doverpublications.com

Day of the Dead Clip Art for Machine Embroidery

In this book you will find a collection of rare, authentic Day of the Dead designs. These images have been carefully chosen, cleaned and prepped to give you the best quality images to use with your electronic embroidery design-making software. This unique publication helps you skip the time-consuming scanning and cleaning of images, and let's you jump right to the fun part—pattern making and sewing out!

What's in the book:

The black-and-white version shows the file that you can use in your design-making program, to create the sewable pattern.

The book is a visual index of all of the files that are on the accompanying CD. In the upper left or right hand corner of each index page are the image numbers that correspond to the equivalent files on the CD.

For every image there are different color ideas for each design.

Next to each color idea is a list of the colors that are used in the design. The number refers to the Isacord thread color number.

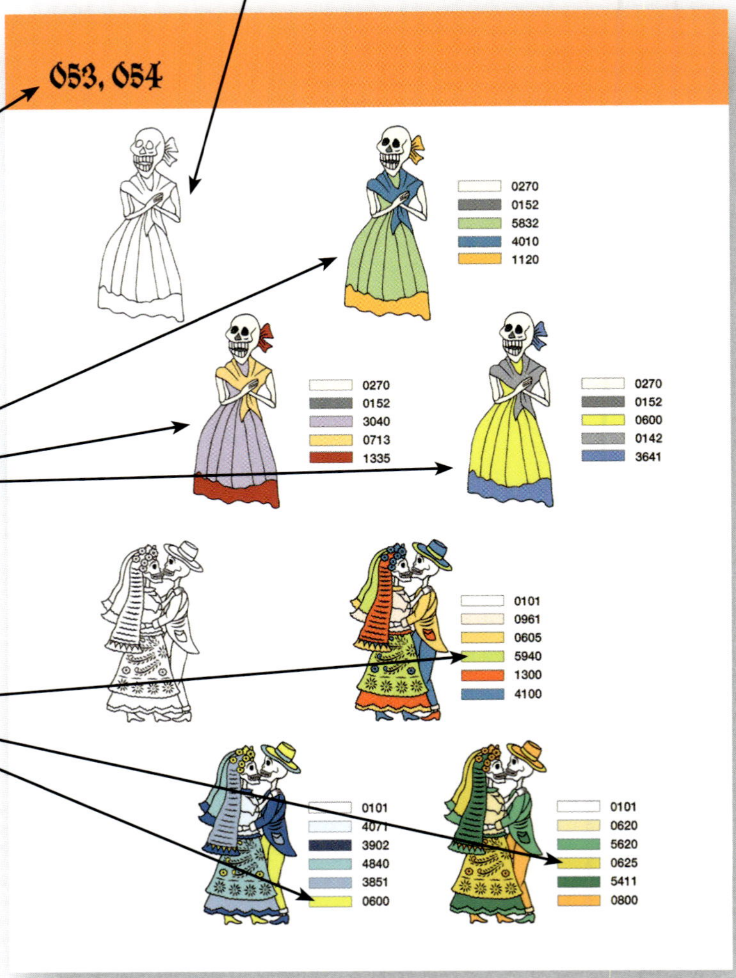

On the inside covers of the book you will find a thread conversion chart, which helps you choose the appropriate thread color from four different manufacturers.

What's on the CD:

There are multiple color versions of each design on the CD. In addition to using them as a source for color ideas, these JPG images can be used as clip art for any crafts or graphics project. These files are located in the "Color JPG" folder.

The black and white versions of the images can be used with most design-making programs to create sewable patterns. There are JPG and vector versions on the CD.

Here is a finished, sewn-out pattern that was made using Brother's PE Design® software program, and Dover clip art.

001, 002

0270
0152
0940
0520
5531
1172
3961

0270
0152
1140
1312
6051
5100

0270
0152
1123
1055
3851
1304
3810

3650
0805
4100
2650
2524

2360
5220
0580
1805
4030

0250
5840
0811
4420
3241

003, 004

0152
0270
3971
3962

0152
3661
0510
0851

0151
1312
0870
0672

0270
0152
3951
0853
4033
1705
0702

0270
0152
1332
1335
0761
5620
5940

0270
0152
3951
0853
4033
1705
0702

005, 006

0270
0152
3262
2910
0713
0853

0270
0152
5610
1532
0874

0270
0152
0805
0941
0904
3901

0270
5020
1099

0270
0610
3251

0270
1304
3842

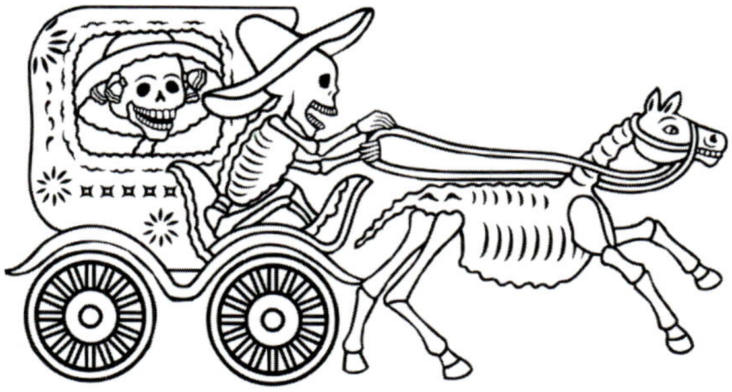

0270
0145
0108
5220
4625
0700
0605

0270
2230
0851
1061
0713
3251
0941

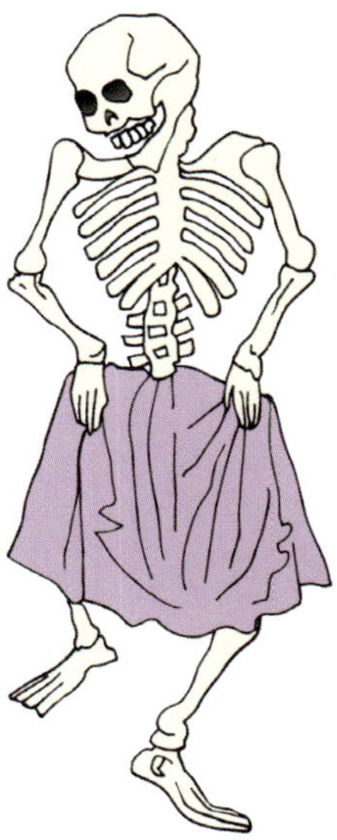

0270
0152
3040

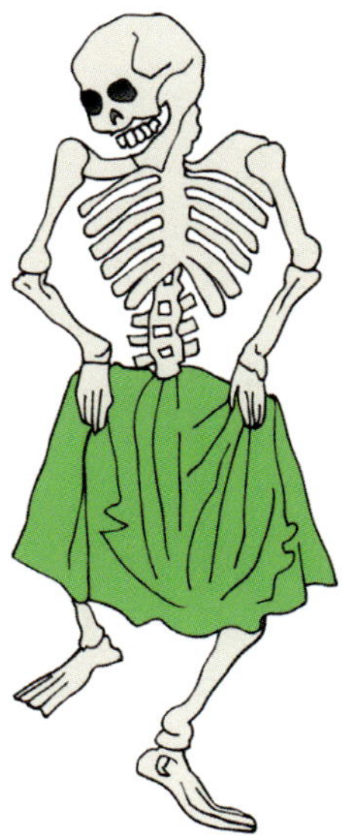

0870
0152
5600

009, 010

0270
0152
0352
0700
0933
0145
0107
1514

0270
0152
5664
0150
0107
0311
3961

0270
0152
3851
1041
1101
3953
0713

0270
0152
1134
0131
4440
1141
0722

0270
0152
1335
0552
1305
0124
5040

0270
0152
5940
0851
5664
0124
0853

011, 012

0270
0152
1102
1115
3750
4105

0270
0152
0702
1914
0761
0873

0270
0152
3262
5500
5324
0713

0270
0152
3640
1705
0934
1905

0270
0152
5050
0142
0904
5210

013, 014

0270
0152
0933
0702
1141
5040

0270
0152
1551
5610
1750
0150

0270
0152
0640
3612
1172
4840

0270
0152
5940
0640
1705

0270
0152
3962
2655
2550

0270
0152
0851
0702
4250

015, 016

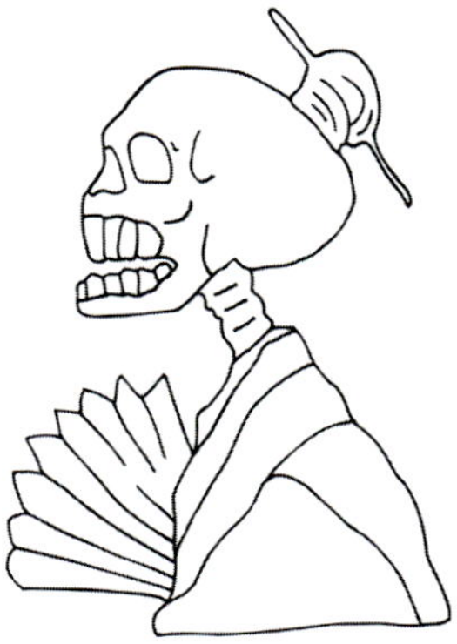

0270
0152
2230
4250
4440

0270
0152
4420
1300
0620

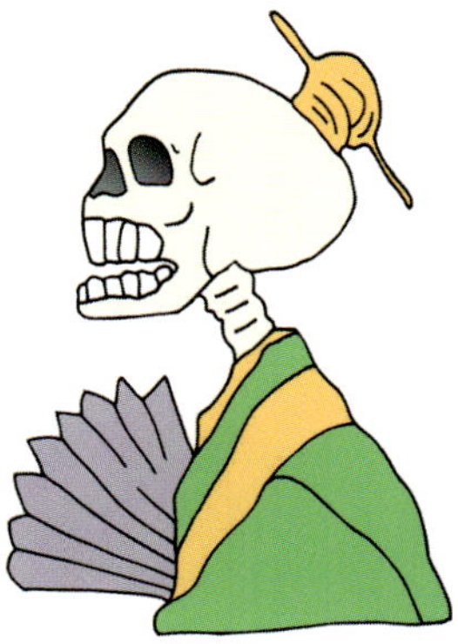

0270
0152
5600
0610
3262

0270
0152
3851
0713
3953
1102

0270
0152
1099
0501
0933
0145

0270
0152
6051
5431
2920
2555

017, 018

0270
0152
2655
2555
5611

0270
0152
5650
3962
3901

0270
0152
5840
0713
1101

0270
0152
1304
5470
1120
0590

0270
0152
2830
4030
3900
1106

0270
0152
0610
4030
1902
2152

0270
3210

3661
1311

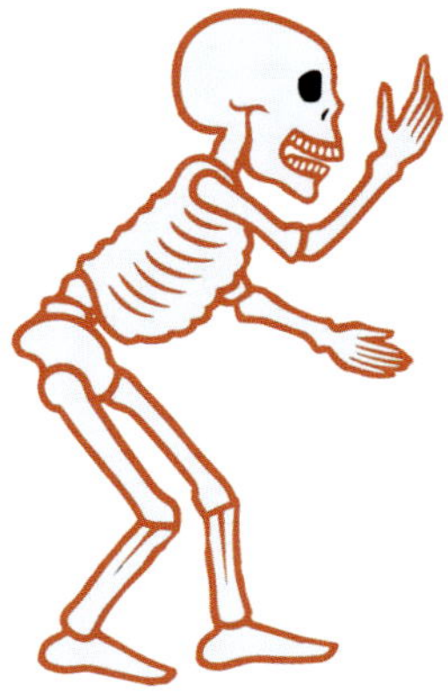

0270
0152
5940
0640
1705
0941

0270
0152
1099
0501
0933
0145

021, 022

0270
0152
3262
0702
3213

0270
0152
4423
4240
1802

0270
0152
0109
5611
5650

0270
0152
1102
1311
0702
3752

0270
0152
5050
5020
2310
0311

0270
0152
3962
3631
0145
4103

023, 024

0270
0152
0933
0702
1141
4840

0270
0152
2230
5510
5940
2166

0270
0152
3901
3961
1320
3543

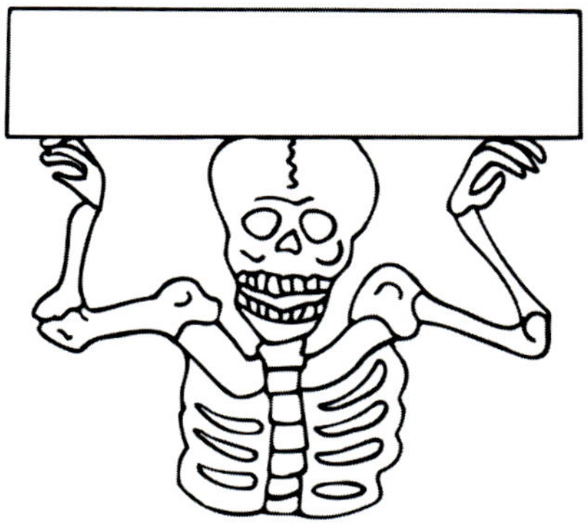

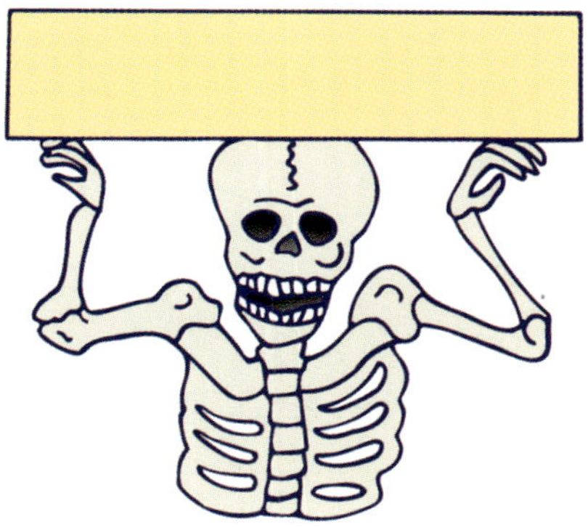

0260
0152
0640
3536

4071
1701
0152
2810

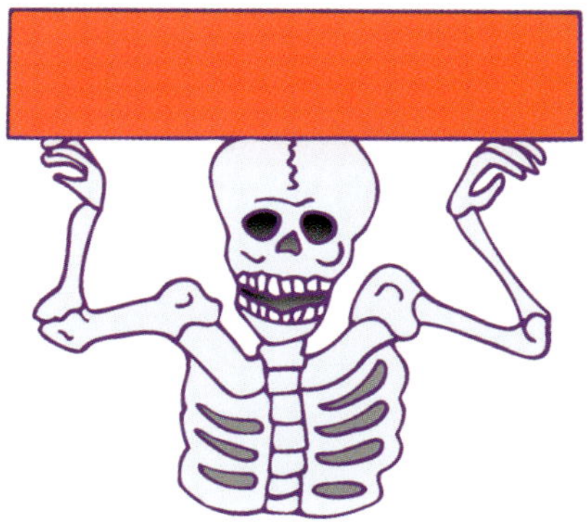

025, 026

0270
0152
0532
5611
4040
4423

0270
0152
0933
1705
0702
1855

0270
0152
2640
0124
2504
0552

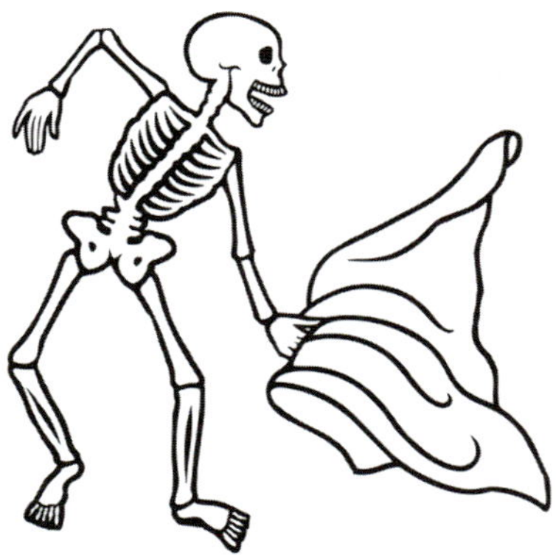

1703
0250

3661
4121

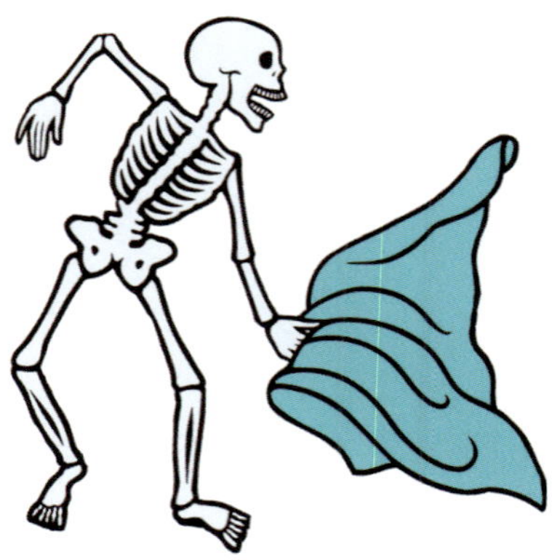

027, 028

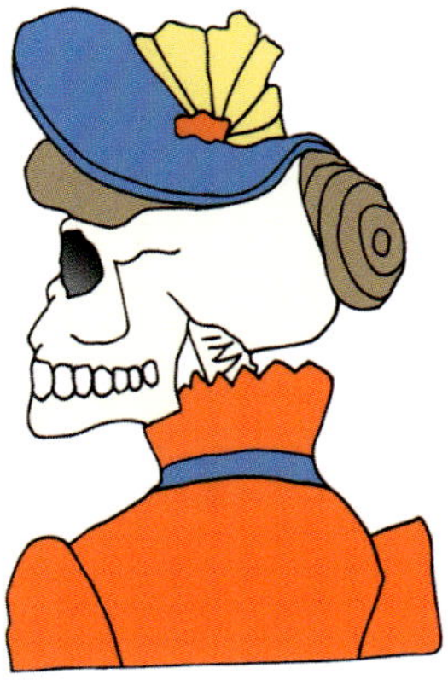

0270
0152
3901
1061
1302
0713

0270
0152
0605
3045
0551
1100

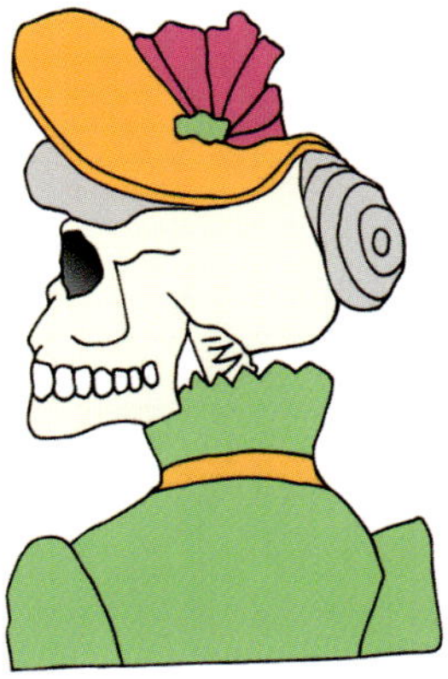

0270
0152
5611
0800
0124
2513

2360
5220
0580
1805
4030

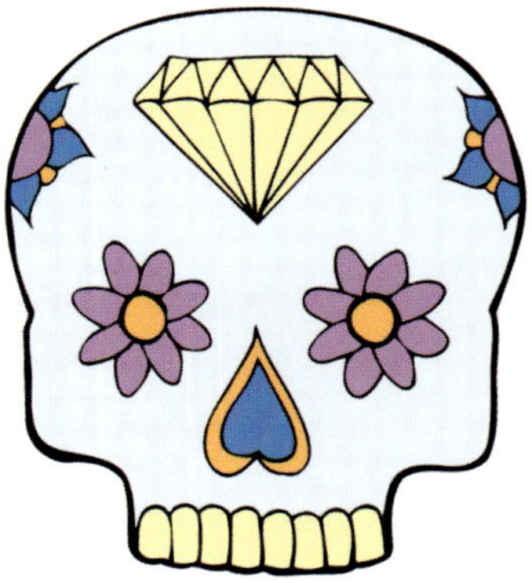

3661
2830
0520
3900
1106

0250
0311
5610
5460
1900

029, 030

0270
0610
1501
5610
5415
2166

0270
0145
0310
4625
2230

0270
3340
5422
0713
1701

0270
0152
0640
3612
1172
4840

0270
0152
0824
5220
0933

0270
0152
1514
1501
3262
1041

031, 032

0270
0152
3851
0713
3953
1102

0270
0152
1312
6051
0904
5100

0270
0152
2645
1172
2920
0713

0270
0152
2230
5510
5940
2166

0270
0152
3851
1041
1101
3953
0713

0270
0152
1304
1532
1120
0590

033, 034

0270
0152
5050
1101
5940
0672

0270
0152
3851
1101
3953
0713

0270
0152
6051
5431
2920
2555

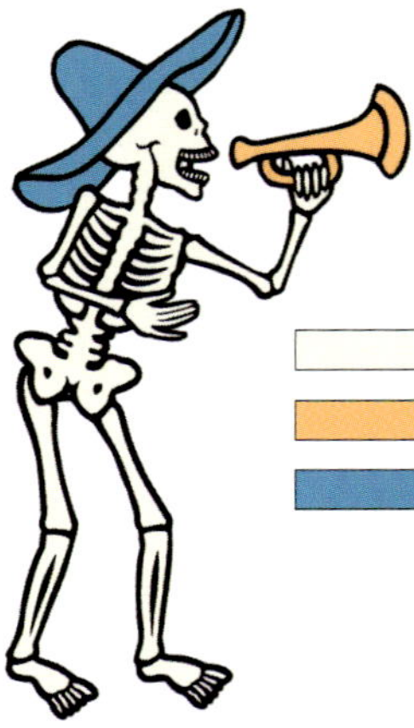

0270
0811
4111

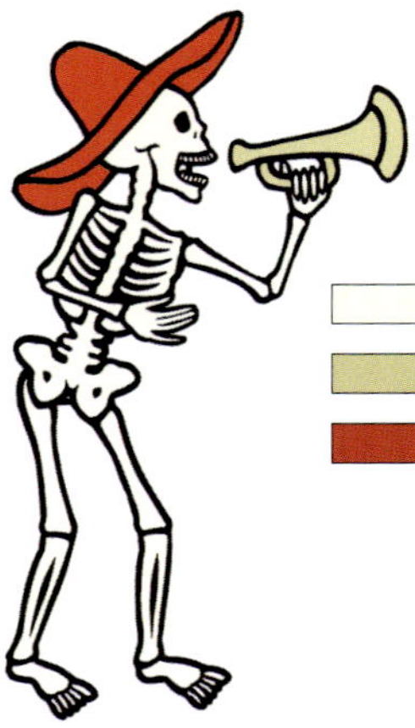

0270
0532
1335

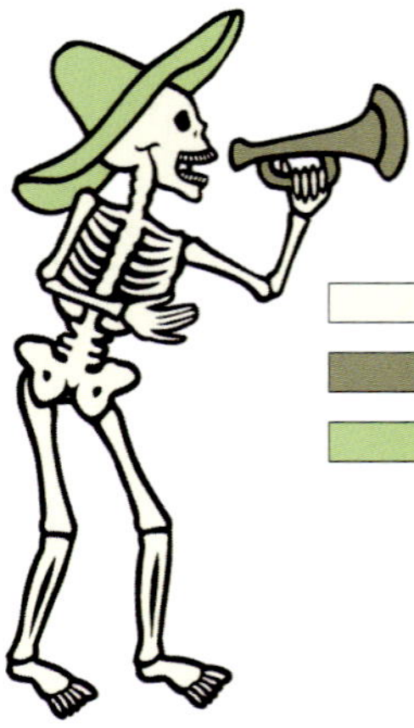

0270
0453
5832

035, 036

0270
0152
5832
5833
5040
0620

0270
0152
3262
0702
3251
0941

0270
0152
1352
1902
0630
4440

0270
0152
0506
3640
3842
0941

0270
0152
5822
0620
1172
1123

0270
0152
4040
0124
1332
1320

037, 038

0270
0152
5611
0800
0124
2513

0270
0152
5940
0640
1705
0941

0270
0152
0702
1914
0761
0873

0270
0822
0726

3661
3951
3952

0270
0182
0605
5415
5940
0532
1902

0270
0580
2830
4030
3900
1106
3770

0270
0152
1430
1335
0761
5620
1302

0270
0152
5610
4105
0713
2513
0109

041, 042

0270
0152
3752
1041
1101
3953
0713

0270
0152
1304
5470
1120
0590
1312

0270
0152
5832
6133
2051
0805
4440

0270
0152
0610
0933
5230
1300

0270
0152
0311
1940
5510
5832

0270
0152
3962
3900
1120
6051

043, 044

0270
0152
1123
5050
1055
1302
5111

0270
0152
2830
4030
3900
1334
2645

0270
0152
0131
0620
0552
3321
1750
1102

0270
0941
0713

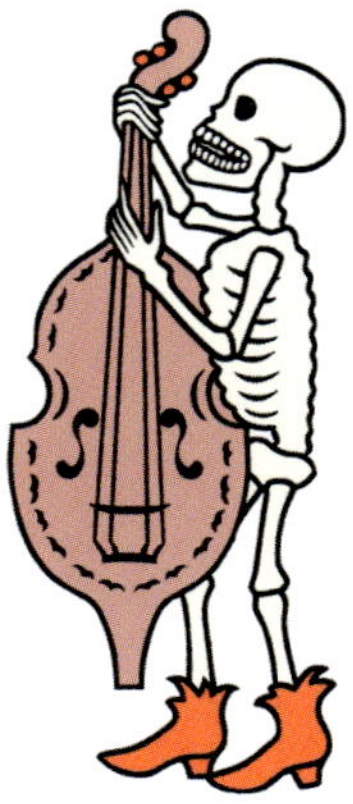

0270
1701
2053

4071
3251
4030

045, 046

0270
0152
1514
1501
3262
1041

0270
0152
3340
5500
5324
0713

0270
0152
0311
3851
3901
0145

0270
0152
0124
0590
2640
3251
5600

0270
0152
5611
0800
0124
2513
1551

0270
0152
0830
0726
3900
0501
0842

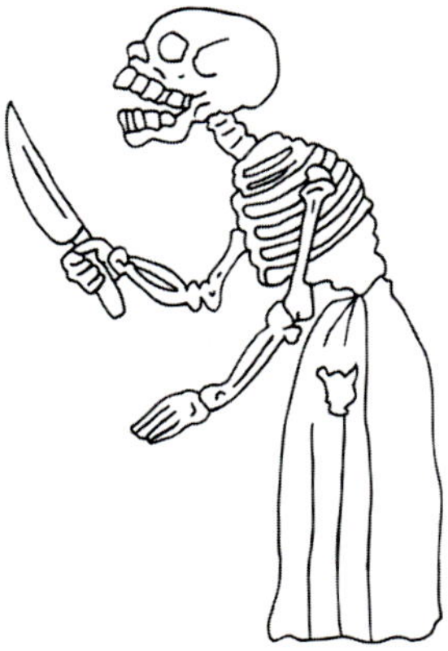

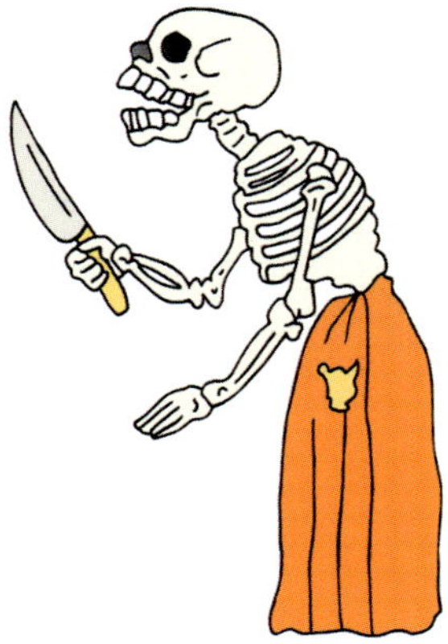

0270
0152
0870
0713
1101

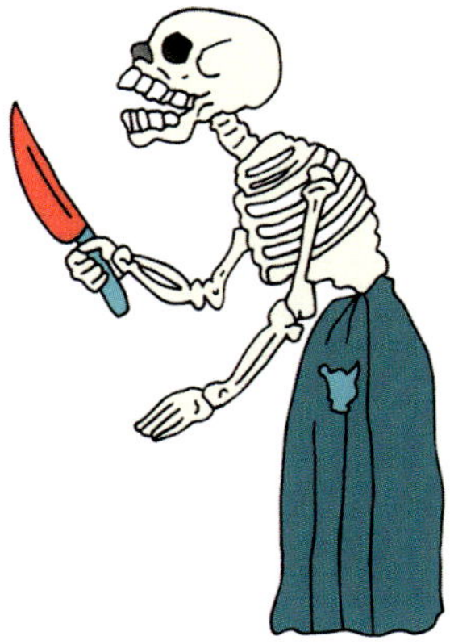

0270
0152
4423
4240
1802

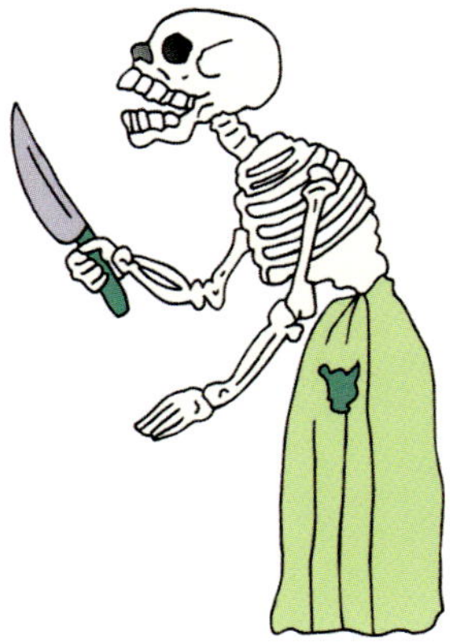

0270
0152
6051
5431
3262

0270
0152
0805
1302
3851
3953

0270
0152
5470
4113
0605
1703

0270
0152
1352
1902
0630
4440

049, 050

0270
5020
0933
0702
1141
5040
5832

0270
0610
1501
5610
5415
2166

0270
0152
1304
3962
1120
0590

0270
0152
5832
5833
5040
0620

0270
0152
2645
0702
3251
0941

051, 052

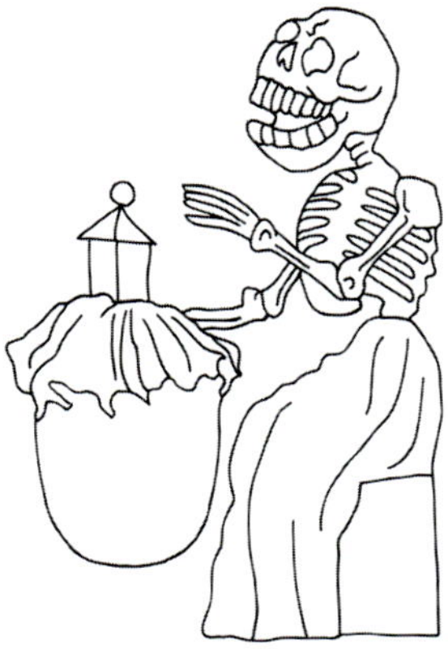

0270
0152
5050
5111
0442
0311

0270
0152
0605
3045
0551
1100

0270
0152
1312
6051
0904
5100

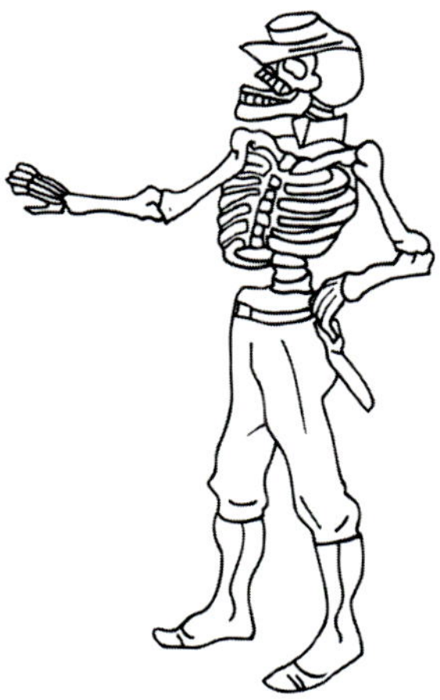

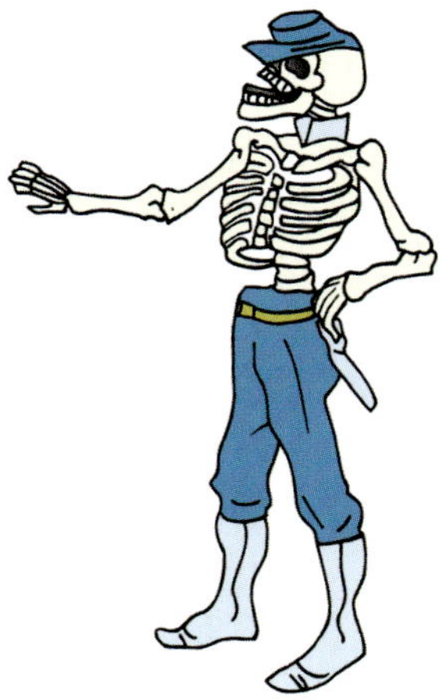

0270
0152
4100
3845
0232

0270
0152
5610
5633
0821

0270
0152
1701
0842
0713

053, 054

- 0270
- 0152
- 5832
- 4010
- 1120

- 0270
- 0152
- 3040
- 0713
- 1335

- 0270
- 0152
- 0600
- 0142
- 3641

- 0101
- 0961
- 0605
- 5940
- 1300
- 4100

- 0101
- 4071
- 3902
- 4840
- 3851
- 0600

- 0101
- 0620
- 5620
- 0625
- 5411
- 0800

055, 056

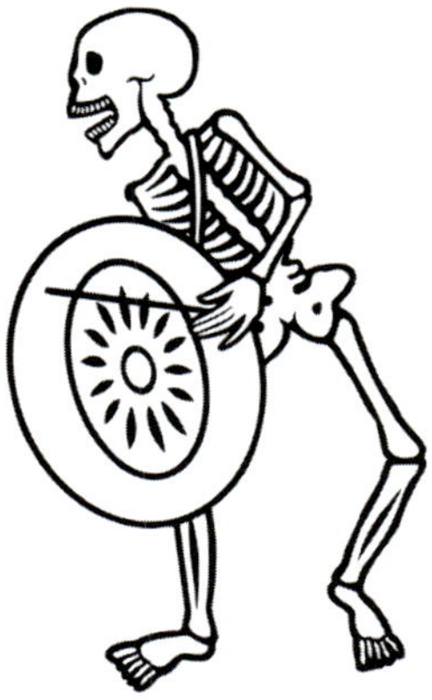

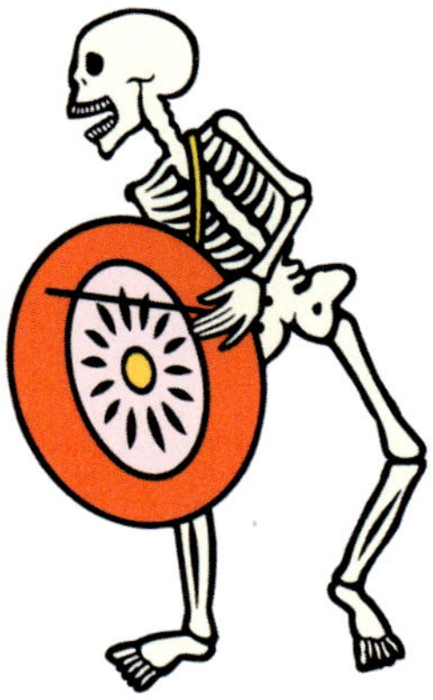

0270
1701
2363
0506

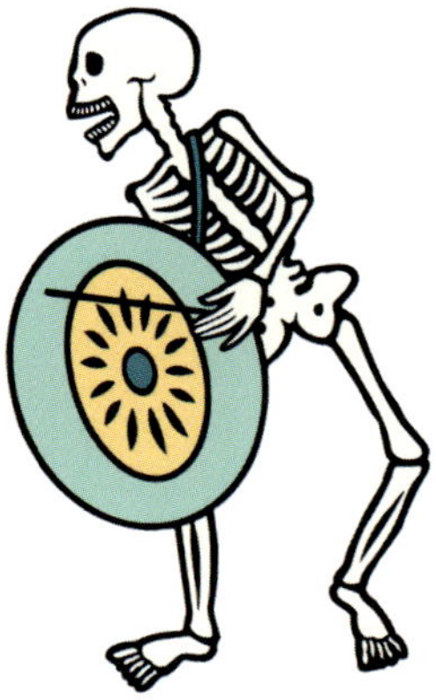

0270
5220
4531
0700

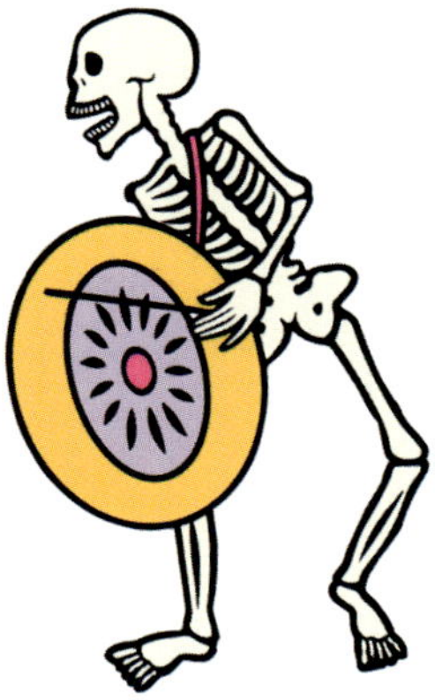

0270
2220
3040
0610

0101
1311
1211
1521

0101
4520
4040
4133

0101
0221
0900
5620

057, 058

0101
0706
0702
0546
1099

0101
0241
2620
0830
2600

0101
1940
2180
1874
1921

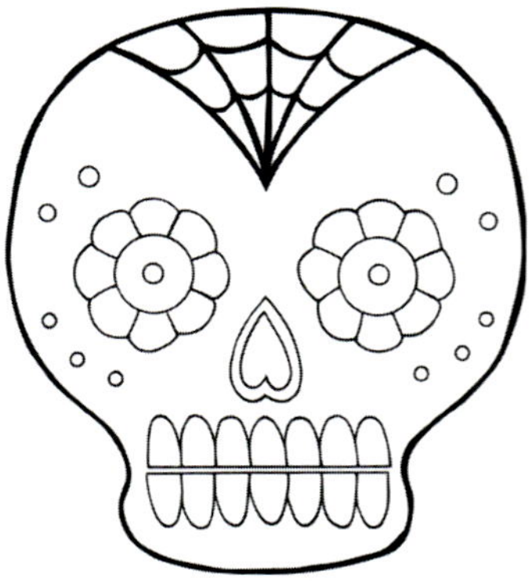

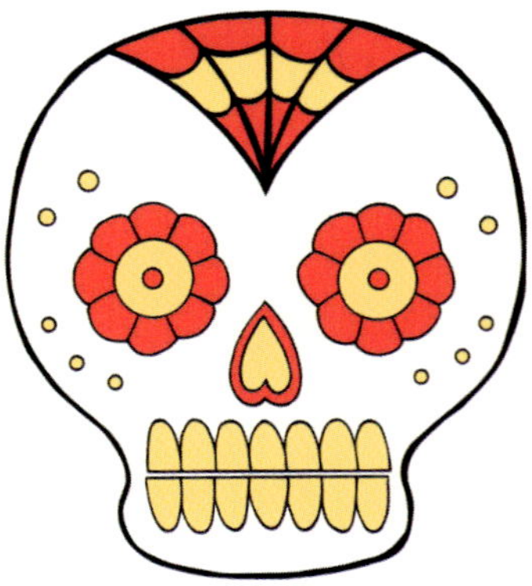

0101
0713
1800

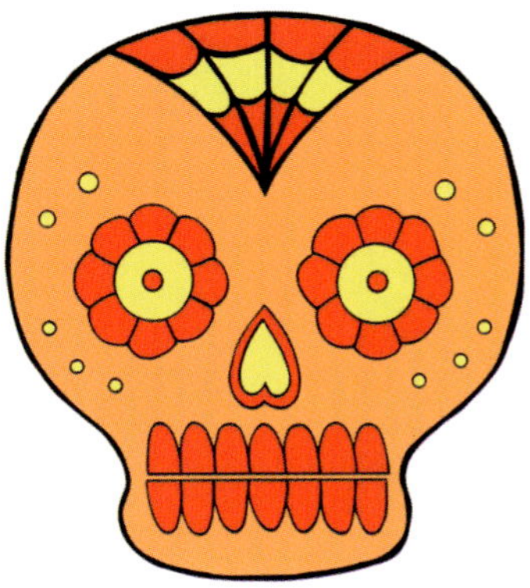

0101
0713
1800

2521
0713
3330

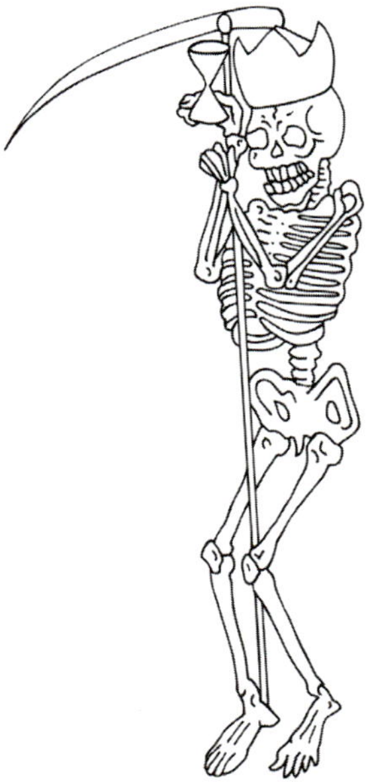

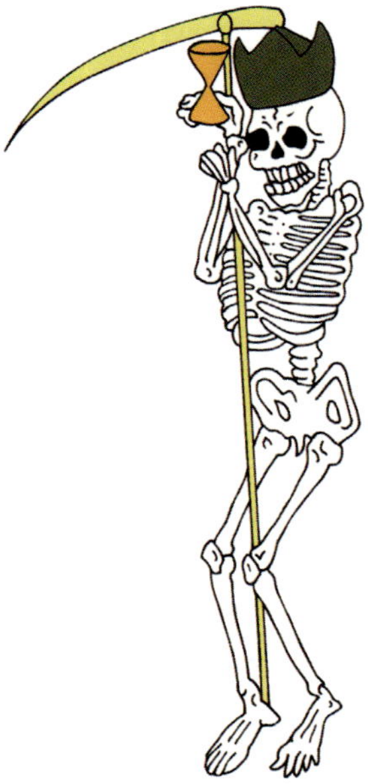

0101
0221
0465
0704

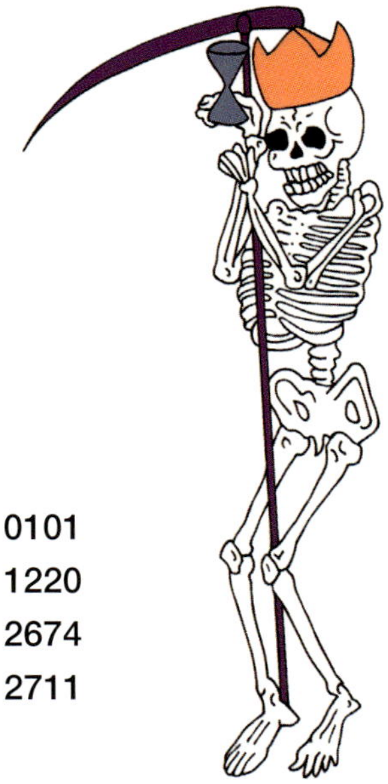

0101
1220
2674
2711

0101
0111
0221
1800

0101
0967
1041
0945

0101
6051
5934
1305

061, 062

5832
2910
1123

1101
5422
1060

4440
4250
3770

2513
5600
0726
2363

3133
1850
5010
0630

063, 064

2165
2300
2905
2743

0620
0232
2220
1366

3845
4040
1102
3210

0270
3641
2820

0101
0811
1840
1421

1313
0101
5940
3333

065, 066

0101
5050
5020

0101
5950
0706

2674
0580
0101
1701

0241
2600
0101
0830

1055
5111
0520
1140

0232
4010
0506
3641

0520
5650
1900
0101

0221
0922
1850
0101

0270
0152
2155
2051
0934
1055

0270
0152
5324
5374
0546
0747

0270
0152
2116
2333
0620
0830

069, 070

1060
0900
1172
0934
1300

0505
0221
0442
0352
0311

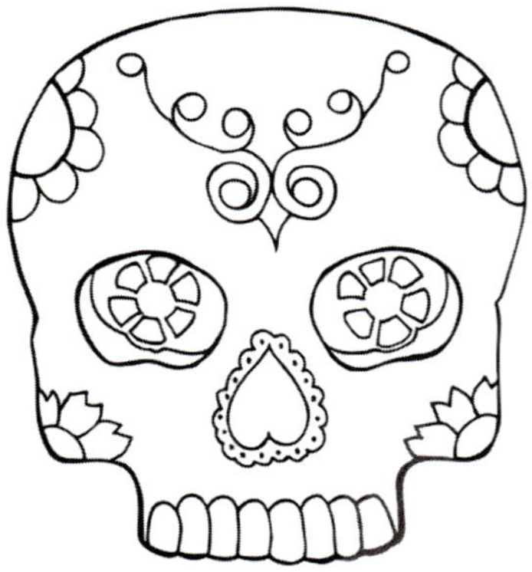

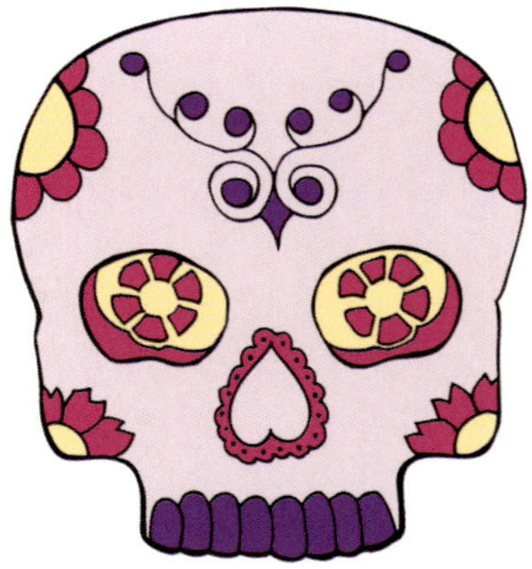

2655
2521
0620
2810

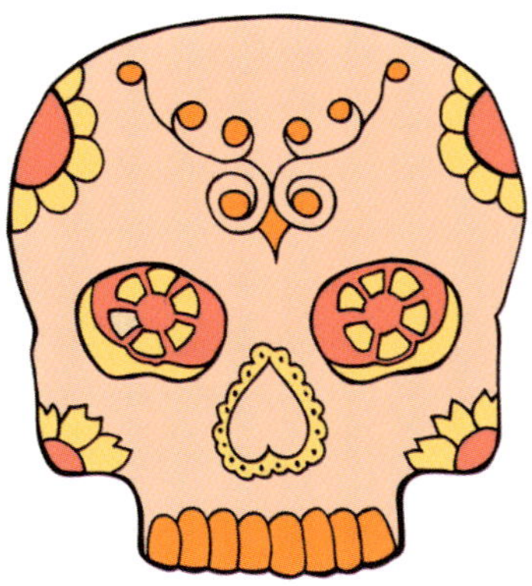

1141
0713
1630
1102

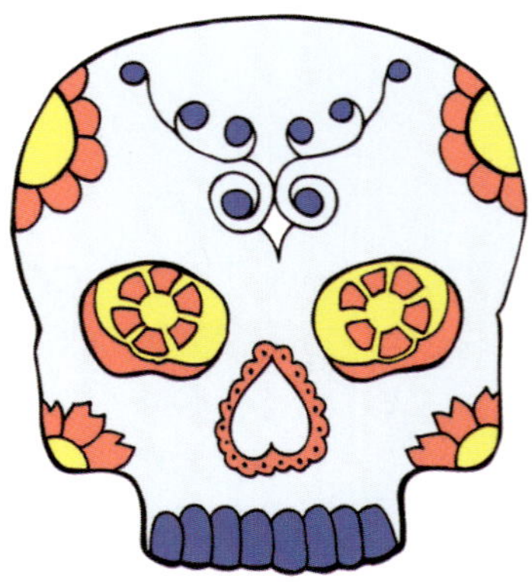

3661
1630
0706
3321

071, 072

0101
0311
1302
1312

0101
5840
5611
3040

0101
1302
1061
1172

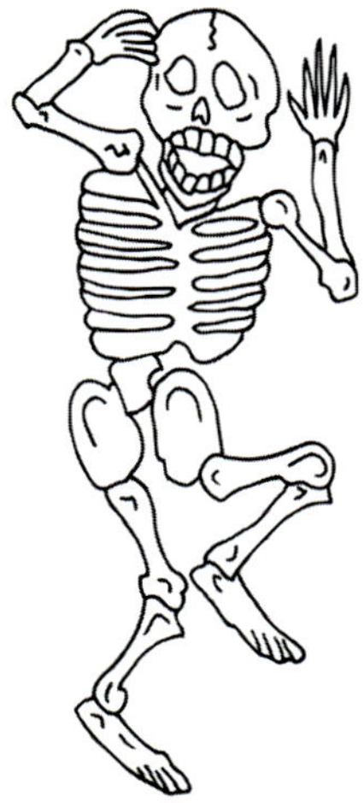

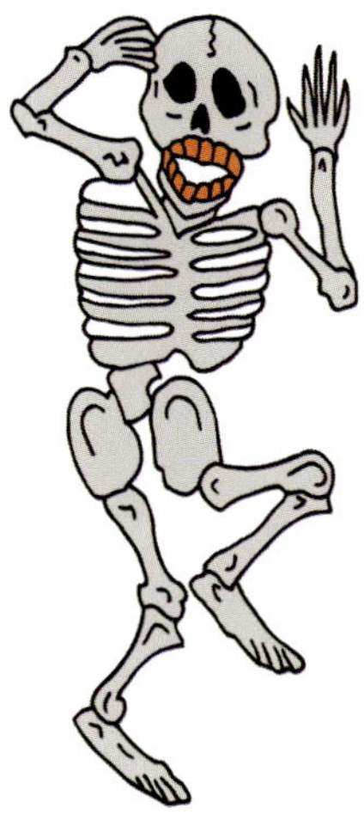

0124
1099
0020

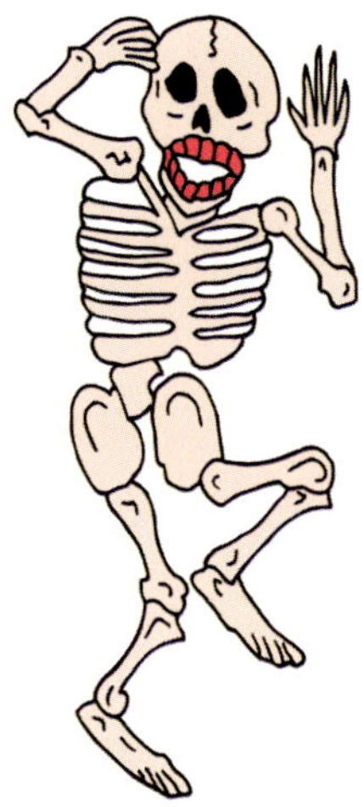

1900
1870
0020

073, 074

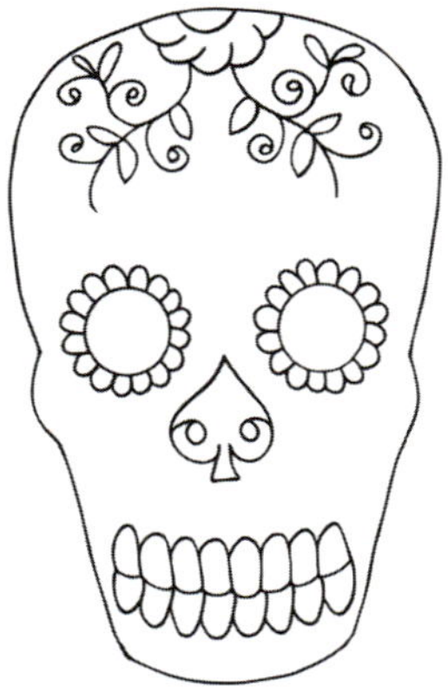

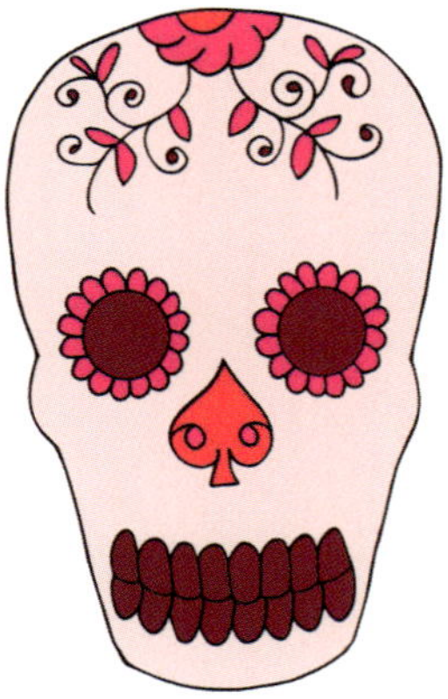

2171
2520
1900
2332

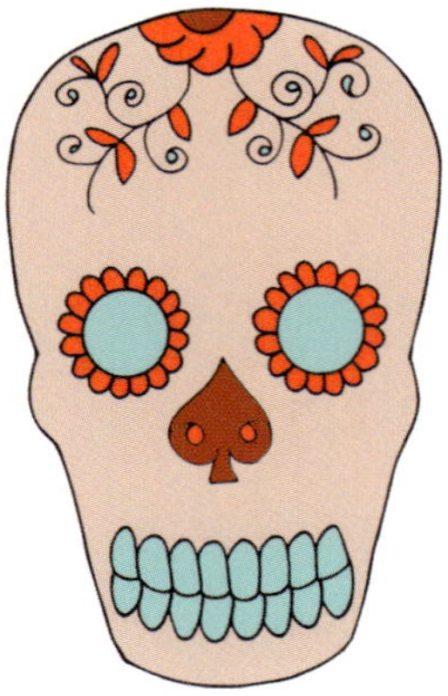

1760
1501
1514
4840

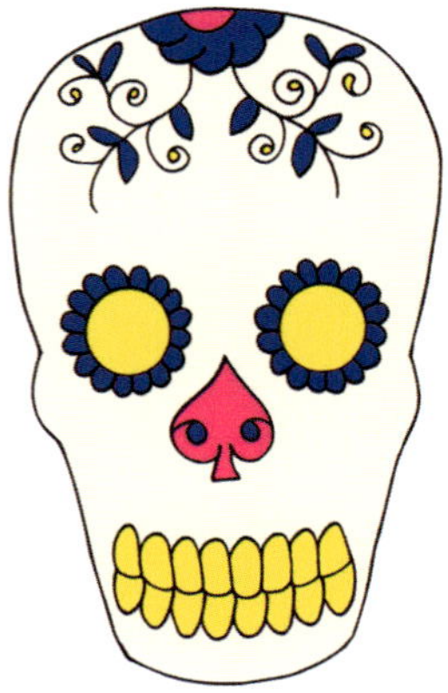

0615
2520
0660
3102

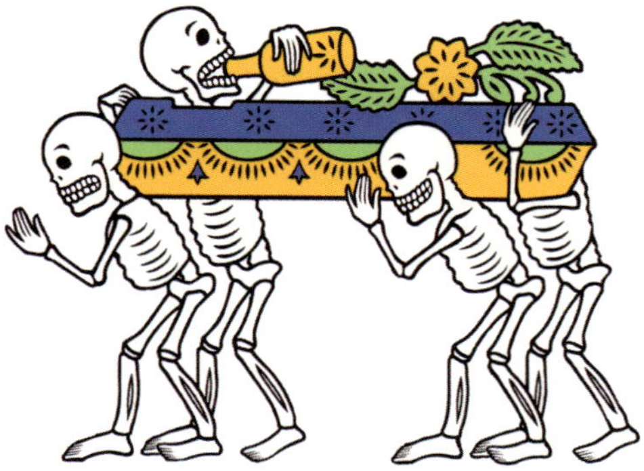

0101
1120
3323
5610

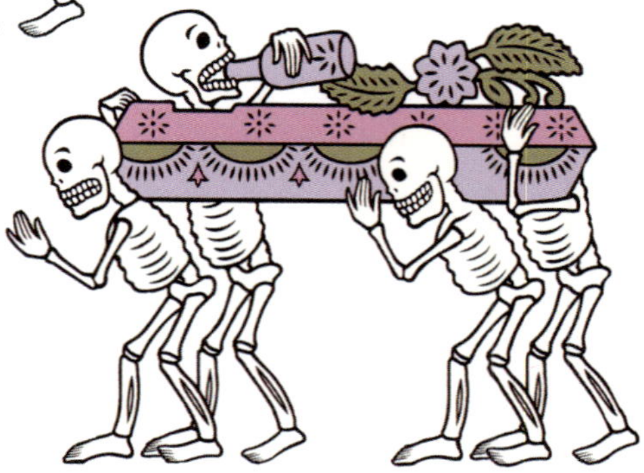

0101
3040
2620
0453

075, 076

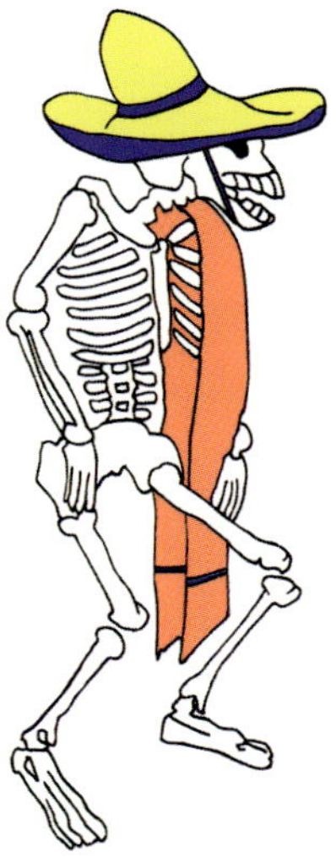

0101
0590
2900
1320

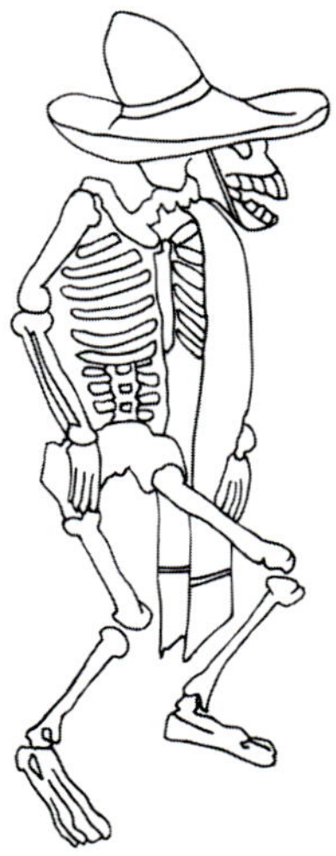

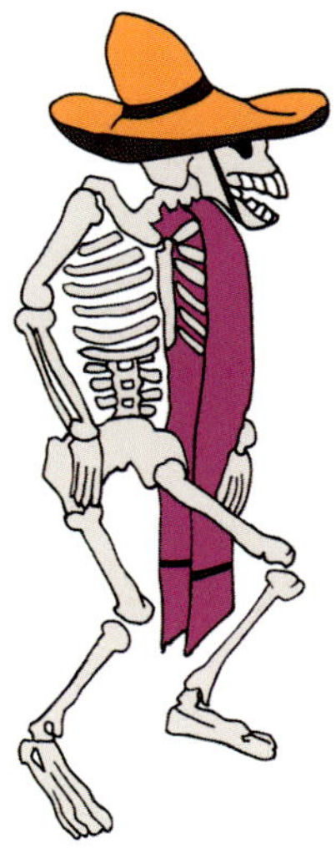

0184
2123
1102
2505

0101
5470
5542
1211
1300

0101
0713
1120
4840
4620

0101
3262
3213
3650
3640

077, 078

0101
0706
4040

0101
2620
0232

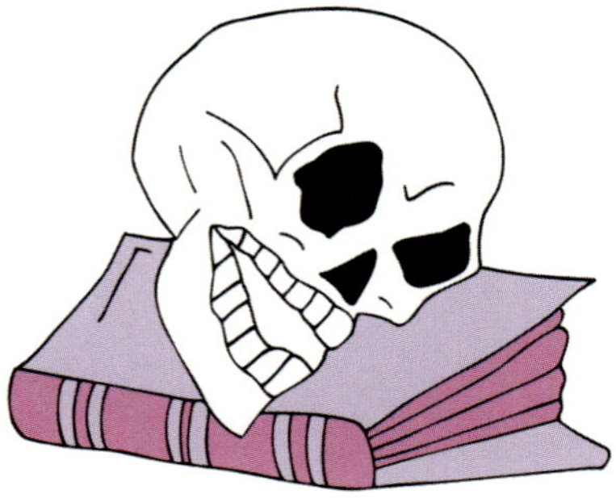

0101
3040
2675

0101
0532
0352
0109
5912

0101
1705
0713
0800
1220

0101
5010
5050
4432
0713

0101
0311
5940
1099

0101
5460
5500
5515

0101
5460
5500
5515
2504

0101
2550
2363
2611
2830

0101
4430
5050
0605
5411

081, 082

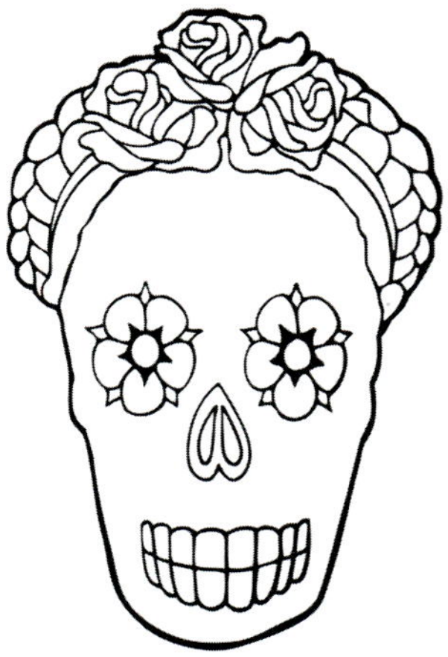

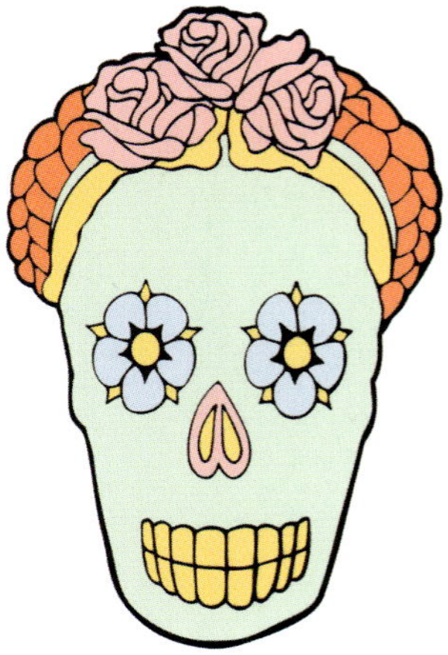

5650
1320
0713
2155
3650

2220
5610
0580
4121

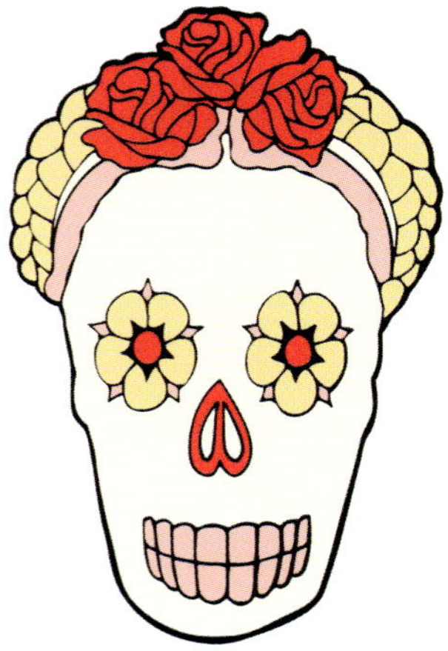

4101
0970
1855
0640

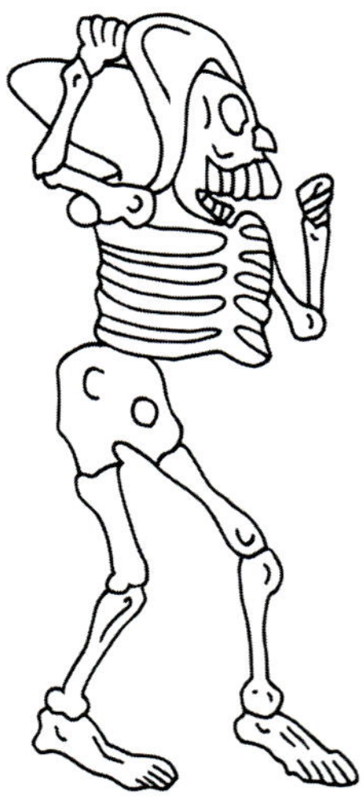

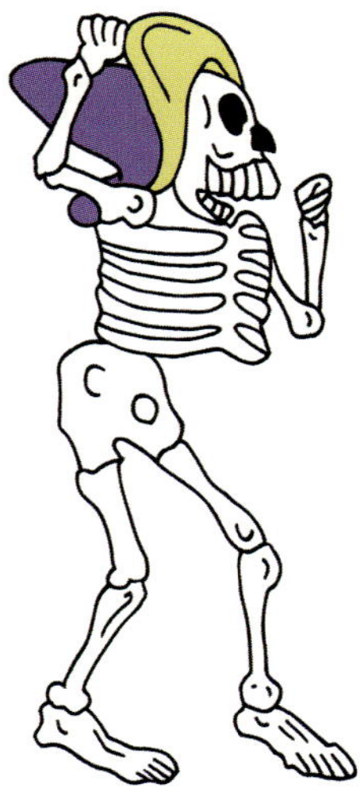

2910
0221
0101

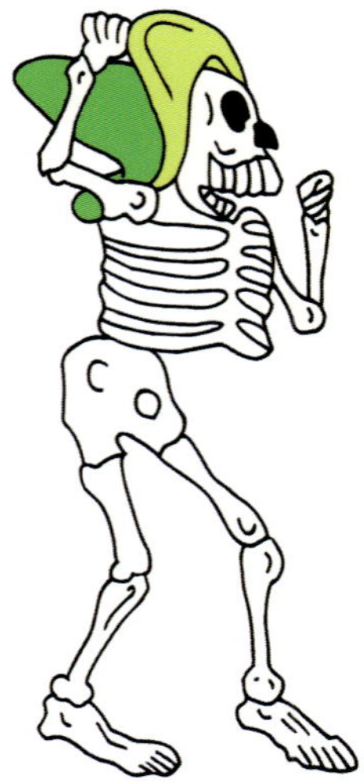

5611
5940
0101

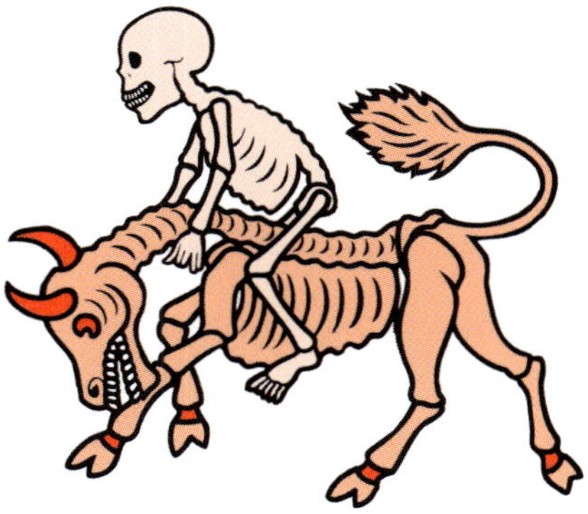

1532
1870
1501

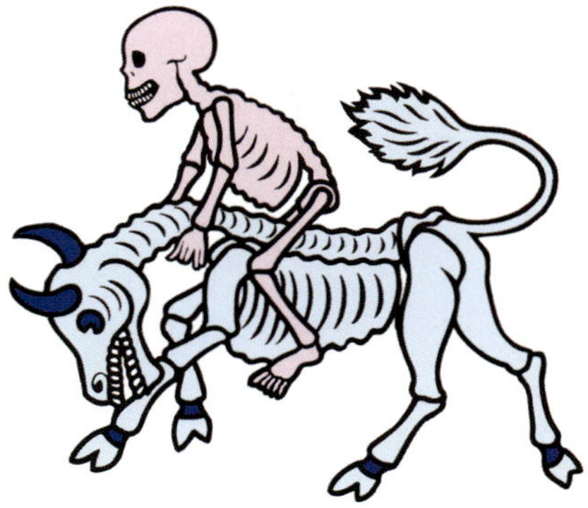

3845
2655
2743

3901
0702
0150
0101

1060
1348
1211
0101

2360
2520
2555
0101

085, 086

0101
2820
1972
0605

0101
3321
1305
0830

0101
4620
2155
4516

1960
0101
1906
2022

5940
0101
0232
0463

0620
0101
1300
0704

087, 088

1140
1355
0101
2011

0221
4840
0101
5000

0805
1211
0101
1348

0270
0152
5832
5833
4250
0620

0270
0152
0610
0933
5230
1300

0270
0152
2230
1914
1760
0310